TIME F(
MY GENERATION
TO DIE

by E.D. Evans
illustrations by Natalie Woodson

Time For My Generation To DIE

Written © E.D. Evans
www.ediedevans.com

Illustrations © Natalie Woodson
Instagram: @nataliewdsn

Edited by Susan Lennox

Photograph on page 9: From the collections of the National Anthropological Archives, Smithsonian Institution

Library of Congress Control Number: 2022912803
ISBN: 9781941573365

Published by Damianos Publishing
2 Central Street, Studio #152
Framingham, MA 01701 USA
www.DamianosPublishing.com

Produced through Silver Street Media by Bridgeport National Bindery, Agawam, MA USA

First printed 2022

TIME FOR
MY GENERATION
TO DIE

by E.D. Evans

illustrations by Natalie Woodson

For all of those I've loved and lost.
For all of those I love who live.

CONTENTS

PART I
WESTERN BALLADS

Saguaro 2
Murder in the First 4
Mexican Lawyer 6
O-O-Dee 8
Jessamine County 10
Monsoon 12

PART II
US NEWS AND
WORLD REPORT

The New Age 16
Paradox in the
    Penitentiary 18
Miss America 20
This Byrd Has Flown 22
Monster Trucks 24

PART III
WHAT PRICE FAME?

Candy and Pills 28
Black Butterfly 30
Whiskey 32
Party Doll 34
One More Fish 36
Sweet Gene Vincent 38
Edie Sedgwick Eulogy 39
Killer Clown, A Lullaby 40

PART IV
TAINTED LOVE

Blues Poem 44
It Rained 46
February 14th 48
The Boy From Hell 50
Jackal, The Conjuror 51

PART V
EASTERN BALLADS

Londontown 54
East Village
    Twelve Stepping 56
Avenue B 59
No Stopping
    the Juice 60
Gone New York
    Gone New York Gone 62
Nowt/Naught 64
Rectify 65

PART I

WESTERN BALLADS

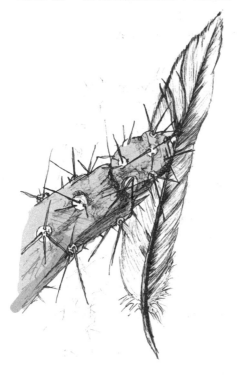

SAGUARO

A Saguaro older than the seas
had this strange tale to tell.
It wasn't just Africanized bees
that made Sonora hell.

Some new gringos rode into town,
their place of choice was many.
The posse, clowns in hand-me-downs,
said, "Here's as good as any."

The Saguaro blinked through narrowed eyes
and scars from birds and bugs.
"You gambling men from far away
are fodder for these thugs."

"I'll watch you gamblers go to Hell.
This much I will avow.
Mi compañeros will not sweat
dead gringos anyhow."

"You'll end up just like all the rest—
Your heads upon a stick.
A harbinger for gambling men,
El Jefe's favorite trick."

El Jefe saw and was not pleased
to see those chollos land.
He forced them down onto their knees
and made them play their hand.

One by one those men were shot,
bullet to back of head.
One by one to the ground they dropped,
A quick dispatch—Then dead.

Each head was placed upon a stick
and raised for all to see—
To warn arriving gamblers,
and as food for the Africanized bees.

They gambled fate and fortune
and filthy lucre sought.
Instead, invited torture
for the trouble that they brought.

Those men with cards and guns and knives
but nothing more in life,
no cheers or kindness, loving blindness,
caress of a wife.

They kept their gambling secrets well,
held closely to their vest.
Until they met El Jefe
who had staked his claim out West.

MURDER IN THE FIRST

Come, gather your children
up close to your vest,
as I tell you a story
of murder out West.

Here follows a tale
about death on the range.
(One might ponder the fact
that so little has changed.)

In old Western times
when wives were commodities,
bloodshed by a woman
would sure be an oddity.

Do not let him fool you—
Nor tell him you care.
He's bad to the bone,
you don't want to go there.

But go there she went,
and shortly thereafter
her soul became bent
and robbed of all laughter.

After he smashed in
her face black and blue
for the fiftieth time,
she knew what to do.
When he lay on his belly,
loud snores from the bed,
she took a steak knife
to his neck and his head.

His skull, it was severed.
She watched him bleed out.
As the sheets spread with crimson,
she spit on the lout.
Then she giggled with glee
at him motionless, dead.
When she kicked him full-force,
on the floor fell his head.

Then she scrubbed all the walls,
and her clothes she did burn.
Light came back to her soul,
and the laughter returned.
So she tidied the kitchen,
then buried the knife.
When the law came, she cried:
"That ranch hand took his life!"

They arrested that man,
but then, at the trial
he cried: "She is the killer!"
The lawyer just smiled.
He reasoned: "No woman
so gentle and kind
could commit such an act
in a rage so, so blind."

The judge and the jury
would only believe
that this delicate flower
could do no more than grieve.
"He's guilty, Your Honor!
For no lady could ever
get away with such murder.
They're just not that clever . . . "

MEXICAN LAWYER

"My life's a bare thread,"
The Vagabond said,
"And my luck is not looking much better.
I took a bad pill.
Can't shrug off this deep chill.
Pulled a string that unravelled my sweater."

I tried and I tried.
Then I lied and I lied.
Ended upside-face-down in the foyer.
"For fucks sake, get help!"
I started to yelp.
I needed an instant deployer.

My thoughts squeaked out sound,
but none were profound.
(At least that's what I told myself, barely.)
I rose up from the ground
where my head had lay down
and looked in the round mirror squarely.

I wasn't so good.
Didn't do what I should.
I rattled and jumped to forget her.
There was never a day
that had started this way
and ended up getting much better.

Life wasn't fair.
I had laid it out bare
when my kindness, instead, did annoy her.
I fell back on the floor—
Where I lay just before
and my lethargy then did destroy her.

Entangled in twine
once soft and divine—
Damp vestiges of a love letter.
My chin jutted down
as I lay on the ground
on the heap of my unravelled sweater.

I left home that day—
(It was better that way)
Gave notice to my main employer.
When the shit I was in
started over again,
I fired my Mexican lawyer.

O-O-DEE

You'd think no one knew how to smile
back in the Old West,
when canyons grand and endless skies
still left most unimpressed.

Sepia portraits of days gone by—
Women with hands folded on their laps,
solemn men look oh-so-shy,
with big, strong jaws and bowler hats.

The Kiowa tribe were beaten down
and forced onto the rez.
Nothing much to smile about
back when Cleveland was Prez.

But then a pretty Kiowa girl
smiled for the camera.
No missionaries saving souls
could gauge that smile's stamina.

She could have been my daughter
when that moment caught her,
smiling for the shot
on that Kiowa spot.

The smell of cordite filled the air.
Not a lot to laugh about back in the day.
The dust was bad, no one could breathe.
Nothing good would come that way.

But a smile belied misery
For just one moment long ago.
A little girl named O-O-Dee,
whose backstory I'll never know.

She could have been my sister
when that moment kissed her,
smiling for the shot
on that Kiowa spot.

For one so young and innocent,
this aftermath was strange.
No one should be able to crack a smile
with life being so tough on the range.

I want to believe she had reason to smile
all those years gone by:
A kiss, or the scent of roasting corn,
or seeing a great owl fly.

An answer I will never know,
buried deep and long ago.
Her secret smile would not reveal
a mystery like bones, so real.

No missionaries saving souls
left a more lasting scripture
than the Great Plains' Mona Lisa,
O-O-Dee's smiling picture.

JESSAMINE COUNTY

Now, this here's a tale, it might sound a bit rough
about trust in the Lord when the going gets tough.

She was mirthful and joyous, a virtuous life,
no lasting attachments—That'd suit her just fine.
No desire for children, was never called "wife",
instead, love for the Lord filled her with the divine.

Then her heart grew despondent, but no one knew why,
and this bleak mood had fell in a manner unkind.
Rocking back and forth slowly, she wished she would die.
When we got there she'd vanished, her keys left behind.

On the desk sat a letter, this only clue read:
"I think about love passing by every day.
I've been dealt a bad blow, and it's done in my head,
and Jessamine County beckons far away."

"I'm going down South, have a talk with my Maker.
The Good Lord knows all, and will show me the way.
I need me some solace, my heart's filled with malice,
I'm going to Jessamine County to pray."

We searched for her low and we searched for her high.
We searched for her every damn day of the week.
We searched 'til our socks soaked with blistering blood
when we found her lying face-down in Jessamine Creek.

We questioned her brother, we talked to the neighbors,
we brought in her pastor—But no one would speak.
Not one gave a reason. It was a sad season
that day she knelt down beside Jessamine Creek.

Mama, don't go down to Jessamine County.
The grass has gone brown and the sun turned to black.
Take your prayers elsewhere, not Jessamine County,
for once you go down there you ain't coming back.

MONSOON

A mournful soul strolled into town.
He came to lay his burden down.
His heart, it sought a place to rest—
This dusty desert town seemed best.

The monsoon came and soon rain fell—
Hail pelted down on desert hell.
A Saguaro swelled with prickly pride.
The traveler's soul inside it sighed.

This lonesome man had gone astray,
played cards to gamble debt away.
He came upon this arid land
where he was dealt a rotten hand.

The monsoon came, and driving rain
flooded dry desert lands again.
A Saguaro swelled with prickly pride.
A gambler's soul inside it cried.

The man he owed rode into town
and shot that traveling gambler down.
The cactus gods gave praise and thanks
and dragged his soul through sawdust planks
into a Saguaro's fleshy crypt.
It lies, entombed between its sticks.
His essence trapped inside it wails,
Release me from this prickly jail!

The monsoon came and soon it went.
It left behind a creosote scent.
A Saguaro swelled with prickly pride.
A mournful soul inside it
curled up and died.

PART II

U.S. NEWS AND WORLD REPORT

THE NEW AGE
(AKA: TIME FOR MY GENERATION TO DIE)

Instant Spirituality is all the rage.
Hello ex-Hippie Boomers: Next stop? The New Age!
Seven Spiritual Laws? Turn the next page.
It's the Word of the Lord for self-centered New Age.
Pseudoscience can kill you, but it's a new gauge,
putting air in the tires of a flaccid New Age.

Look for a master, a monk or a sage,
he'll show you the path to a pricey New Age.
Learning enlightenment? Spend your last wage—
Put it smack in the pocket of a Guru New Age.
Zen Master Money frees you from your cage in
one-thousand-dollar suits in late Boomer's New Age.

They feast on the needy and those who've lost hope.
They make lots of money off those who can't cope.
But it's better than TV—Reality soap.
It's cocaine for the sheeple and stronger than dope.

Well into middle age and still can't find Nirvana?
Why not go to Sedona and rent your own Bwana?
Used to like tripping, but now Prozac's your acid?
There's the spiritual store . . . Slow down, wait!
Damn! . . . You just passed it!

Replace your religion with even more useless knowledge
than could ever be found in "The Earth is Flat" college.

Adapting a language for new platitudes that
sanction a host of unreal attitudes?
Like "The Universe—It will provide."
(Rational self, kindly step to the side.)

So when chanting for money is what you lean toward,
and reading *The Secret* tells you that you've scored,
could it be you're scared shitless of just being bored?
And contemplation of death leaves you utterly floored?

Advice: Make a crop circle while burning your sage
that says "Eat me, I've sinned in this stinking New Age."
Opiate for the masses—The old Boomer's rage.
It's old and it's over.

Goodbye, fucked up New Age.

PARADOX IN THE PENITENTIARY

When Martha Stewart served her time,
it forced a change of style.
Her happy hostess persona
took backseat for a while.

Reduced to dirty grunt work,
and her cellmate was a whore,
she missed her friend, Snoop, something bad
as she lay on the cold cement floor.

Banana bread, banana bread,
it is so soft and sweet.
I miss baking banana bread.
That bread is such a treat!

I promised Snoop banana bread
next time he came to visit...
Snoop Dogg reminds me every day,
banana bread's the Shizzit.

The days went by but nothing changed—
No oven at her disposal.
Banana bread was on her mind.
She had a new proposal:

"If I were to bake banana bread
Just one time for you, Guard,
perhaps an extra privilege,
such as more time in the yard?"

The guard replied, (and Martha sighed),
"You just can't bake in prison.
If I let you bake banana bread
there'd be a great division."

Regardless, Snoop Dogg got no bread
and smoked his blunt alone.
No Martha Stewart gangsta-style.
No bread to call his own.

So Martha had to wait, instead,
until her time was served.
She never baked banana bread,
but got what she deserved.

MISS AMERICA

I want to be Miss America:
Wear a cheesy tiara, and let your host, Donald Trump,
not so secretly grab my bikini-clad pussy
as I waltz down a gang-plank
while singing a vocally-challenged rendition of
Let it Go.

I want to be an American tragedy—
Dye my hair Marilyn Monroe bleach blonde,
first-degree-burns searing through my scalp
while eating the Hostess "American Dream" Twinkie.

I want to pump NRA iron
to perk up my bullet-boobs.
I want to wear red, white and blue make-up
that will harm furry little creatures
and give me skin diseases.
I want to don star-spangled high-heels
that will encourage slipped discs.

I want to wolf down the American Bacon Burger.
Then, I want to retch it up discreetly
into the lap of a toilet in some
spotless orange and yellow McRestaurant.

I want to voraciously consume
Cosmo, Marie Claire and *Vogue.*
Then, according to their fine advice columns,
I want to hire a team of spelunkers
to explore my vaginal walls with flashlights,
searching for my G-spot like a lost Atlantis.

I want a taste of the
American Jacqueline Daniels dream.
She feels so good
cruising down my Highway 1,
Route 66 pink Cadillac gullet,
and so God-bless-her,
love-it-or-leave-it bitter
coming back up.

THIS BYRD HAS FLOWN

She was stuck in Yucca Valley
when the two of them met there.
His daddy was so famous
that he didn't have a care.

Comingling in the desert,
they were both drunk as skunks.
He told her who his daddy was.
She had her a slam-dunk!

He was nothing but a loser,
grew up in the shadow of fame.
He was just a worn-out boozer,
but he still had Daddy's name.

Because Daddy was an icon—
A heavy weight to carry.
But she'd be a celebrity
if him she were to marry.

Once she worked the sex trade.
Blow jobs paid the rent.
Now that she had married up,
her life she'd reinvent.

She played guitar bare-fingered
and sang a warbly song.
They say she's a dead ringer
for everything gone wrong.

Her $1000 Wedding—
How long did she have to stay?
It felt more like a funeral.
It was a bad, bad day.

Although she looked quite innocent,
she had a convict's smell.
She used him and abused him.
Made his life a living hell.

She wrapped him 'round her pinky
and left him in the dust.
Though her consciousness was kinky,
she still wanted Daddy's trust.

So, she moved to a shack in Arkansas—
It was shitty, old and ratty.
However, it was much closer to
her husband's famous daddy.

She kept his famous surname—
For she could not resist.
'Til Daddy's lawyer called her
and said "Cease and Desist."

She played him like a fiddle
right down to the last note.
And therein lies the riddle—
She became the country song she wrote.

MONSTER TRUCKS

MONSTER TRUCKS gonna getcha.
MONSTER TRUCKS bigger than the Empire State Building.
MONSTER TRUCKS bigger than the Grand Canyon.
MONSTER TRUCKS bigger than the Universe.

MONSTER TRUCKS make me wanna do wild things,
crazy things,
reckless things
like shave my head.
Like play mumblety-peg between your legs.
Like get a tattoo of a behind on my behind.
Crazy, crazy, MONSTER TRUCKS.

MONSTER TRUCKS make me wanna do naughty things,
secret things,
nasty things,
like have wet dreams about protective facial gear.
Like cashing my dead mom's stimulus check.
Like drinking a hydroxychloroquine cocktail.
Sexy, sexy MONSTER TRUCKS.

Me, I sit so proud in my tall bleacher seat,
my GRAVE DIGGER, OVERKILL, BIG FOOT, EXCALIBER
T-shirt newly blessed with
mud, beer, and blood.

Me, I come from the land of the
American Gladiatin' car-crushin'
stage divin' mud wrastlin' Maga Dawg riotin'
rockabilly shockabilly cockabilly
MONSTER TRUCKS,
and my tires are
SO BIG.

PART III

WHAT PRICE FAME?

CANDY AND PILLS

At first that pill was fine and tasty,
like a sucker candy.
A sweet, sweet pill; a deadly thrill—
A rare Kentucky Brandi.

It tasted of hot kisses—
Not of psychic consternation.
It promised tender roads ahead—
Not icy marginalization.

Sweet sucker pill melted in his mouth.
Sweet sucker pill melted on his tongue.
Sweet sucker pill took him way down South.
Sweet sucker pill was easy to swallow
when he was young.

He took that pill day in and out,
the candy taste grew bitter.
It stuck strong deep inside his throat,
but he could not, would not, quit her.

He only wanted candy,
not a bitter pill to swallow.
And like Kentucky Brandi,
it left him rare and hollow.

Might be a crooked road's twisted fate.
Might be laced with straw-yellow hair.
Might be a burden too heavy and wicked.
Might be an old lead foot
heard on the stair.

Being stoic breaks a man,
but being human makes a man.
Sad, those songs never made a sound
before they ever had a chance
to hit the ground.

BLACK BUTTERFLY

Driving my short bus, what do I spy?
Why ain't that a big old black butterfly!
I can't seem to shake it outta my sight,
black butterfly follows me day and night.

Hey, add this song to the band's set list!
Don't ask me how it goes or I'll get pissed.
Oh, you want to hear it now? Nah, I'll play it later—
Right after I wrassle this here alligator.

He tried to make me happy, famed, and knowing.
That's when my diva wings started showing.
At the big trade show the real one to catch
was me drunk on the floor advertising my snatch.

Went to a funeral, it was so wrong—
At the gravesite forced to hear another man's song.
Why'd he get to sing instead of me?
Every common drone knows that I'm the Queen Bee!

Now I'm running 5Ks with nowhere to go,
career's in the loo on Kentucky Skid Row.
I cast my lot with a ginger loser
and ended up a porcine boozer.

Honey Jack finally got the best of me.
Don't look, there ain't nothing left to see.
No matter, I'll destroy his life
and scare away his future wife.

My drunken nightmares reveal to me
the dusty trail of a Dixie Bee.
Blew my chance to catch that star.
Now I'm not even making tips from a coffee jar.

Mid-life crisis—Shit, what is it?
Choco-lonely pays a visit.
Limelight crashed to the floor with a thud.
Squandered dreams . . . shoulda stuck with Bud.

WHISKEY

When I woke up in the afternoon,
I looked at the blur in the mirror.
I spewed up in the sink.
Then I had me a drink
and it started becoming clearer.

Whiskey, she's my mother.
She birthed me in a stink.
Then she gave me her breast,
and you know the rest—
I had me my first drink.

For all these odd years of my life
the lines on my face don't lie.
I put away twenty bottles a day,
and I know that I'm going to die.

Whiskey, he's my father.
He brought me to the bar.
He fed me a whiskey,
and when I got frisky,
he threw me the keys to the car.

Can I stand up for a minute
or will I fall down on the floor,
lose my money once again,
and smash my face into the door?

Can I make it through the encore?
Can I make it to the show?
Can I stay sober for an hour?
Do I really have to go?

Whiskey, she's my lover.
She's soft and golden-brown.
She spits fire on my lips
when we first kiss,
then she's smoother going down.

Someday soon I'll soar straight to Hell
in a DC-7 black and white,
cry goodbye in my glass,
and fall on my ass
in preparation for the flight.

You see, I'm not alone in this cockpit
with the steering wheel and throttle.
My co-pilot's sitting next to me—
And he's a bottomless whiskey bottle.

PARTY DOLL

Bobby, Jack, and Marilyn
dance up in Heaven.
Sex and drugs and suicide
notwithstanding.

Bob and Jack were sleazy.
Marilyn was easy.
Chewed her up and spit her out,
and so, her love got greedy.

Marilyn's insatiable.
JFK's replaceable
by his little brother's dick.
Bobby was agreeable.

Marilyn was pleasing.
Jack and Bobby, teasing.
It seemed like rape from Hoffa's tapes.
The whole thing smelled of treason.

Presidential policy
was a hot commodity.
Marilyn used and then abused.
It wasn't such a novelty.

Handsome, roguish Kennedys
forced Miss Monroe to her knees,
bobbing up and bobbing down
on Jack and Bob to please.

Marilyn's last phone call:
Lawford just ignores it all.
Words are spoken, heart is broken,
but the dinner party's still a ball.

Marilyn Sex Goddess,
flirtatious and immodest,
died in her bed (that's what they said.)
She was alone, regardless.

Jack and Bobby's party doll.
They both stood by and watched her fall.
Happy Birthday, Mister President . . .
. . . And praise the Lord for Nembutal.

ONE MORE FISH

Tennessee skies are cold and grey
one early Sunday morn.
The lake reflects your tired fate.
It's time to move along.

As in a dream, an arc of fish
breaks through the surface clear.
One jumps up and one jumps down,
not going anywhere.

They jump over and over, one than the other,
over and over again.
Count one than the other, then one than the other,
then stop, then start again.

Just one more fish, just one more fish
might keep a brain from humming.
Just one more fish, just one more fish.
You knew this day was coming.

Tried hard to make it, just couldn't stay,
Lyfting your whole life away.
Now Nashville's time has come and gone,
replaced by corporate Amazon.

The fish jump over, one than the other,
over and over again.
Count one than the other, then one than the other,
then stop, then start again.

It took its toll and wrecked a soul:
Music City got the best of me.
I'm on my way where skies aren't grey
and lizards race, Westerly.

Those fish go jumping up and down
and land without a splash or sound.
Just one more fish—You counted ten
just jumping up and back again.

Their scaly frames jump up then down,
over and over again.
Count one than the other, then one than the other,
then stop, then start again.

Just one more fish, just one more fish
might keep a brain from humming.
Just one more fish? A squandered wish.
You know that day ain't coming.

Tried hard to make it, just couldn't stay.
Lyfting your whole life away.
Now Music City's come and gone.
Adios Cartel Amazon.

Movin' on.
Gone to stay.
Vaya con Dios, Mi Compa.

SWEET GENE VINCENT

Bop makes you rockin', Bop makes you mean.
Ain't nothing dirty that's never been clean.
The beat was the Bop, it was sin and rage
that dragged his metal-braced leg right across the stage.

Back down on Bop Street where Eddie sang,
Elvis, Carl, Jerry Lee would hang.
They could all do the Bop—Sexy, cool, and lean,
but none could Be-Bop-A-Lu like my Sweet Gene.

He lived too fast and died too old.
He lost a race with the Devil and he sold his soul.
His metal-braced leg glared off the light.
His kisses still touch me in the middle of the night.

Sweet Gene, you were never meant to stay.
Your liver gave out on Judgement Day.
But when you were young, and sleek, and mean—
Man, you dragged your metal-braced leg
right across my dreams.

EDIE SEDGWICK EULOGY

Twisted little elf
stolen off the shelf.
Seen too much wealth
for your own good.
Face full of grace stares into space,
dying in your sleep
like you knew you would.

Plenty of regality,
glamor and reality
just don't mix—
They can't be bought.
Once there was beauty
but face turned puffy,
autistic child without a thought.

Ass like a battlefield,
arms like a drag race,
Atlas road map is your skin.
Andy Warhol calling.
Andy Warhol balling.
Open up your bedroom door
and let Andy in.

Throwaway society,
pillbox anxiety,
a click of the camera—
Now you're in the majority.
Funny little Edie,
twisted, dumb, and speedy,
all for Andy Warhol's coercive priority.

KILLER CLOWN, A LULLABY

Who would believe the evil
that lurks in the hearts of shadowed men?
Who would believe such trying times?
(Really, only them.)

Let's chat about Misfits who creep
into our lives and the skid marks they leave.
Hush little one, now get some sleep.
Guess what? It's time to heal and grieve.

Well HELLO THERE, Killer Clown.
Take a bow from Hell!
Show us what you got before you rot,
Gosh golly gee—that's swell!!!!!

Slice 'em like Tyson, elicit a frown.
Deception's a mighty power base.
Chop 'em, dice 'em, don't let us down!
Then scarper behind your painted face.

That clown is six feet 'neath the ground,
and no longer creeps about when late.
So, go to sleep and dream some dreams
you wouldn't wish on those you hate.

The boy's now a man who does not hide.
Consider this delayed revenge.
He never asked, and he never lied.
Mind the Gap: Don't touch Stonehenge!

These days he has a lot to say.
Fear can't stake claim on artistic plains.
Though visions haunt him every day,
clowns can't mine gold in protected veins.

HEY!
This cowardly shite who had no might—
You'll never be his slave.
Repeat this mantra as you stand
pissing on his grave:

Once you robbed my right to fight—
But never my industrial-strength will.
And your heinous visage on my knee
soothes more than any pill.

PART IV

TAINTED LOVE

BLUES POEM

I want to feel your love,
but my love's in vain.
You got one foot on the platform
and the other on the train.

I see our faces in the mirror,
and they're lined with pain.
You got one foot on the platform
and the other on the train.

You gotta make up your mind.
It's what you gotta do
'cause this train will start to roll,
and you'll be ripped in two.

I could make it easy for you,
say we made a mistake.
But I'd rather stick around
just to see you break.

You see, it's heading down South
over dry, dead plains
when you got one foot on the platform
and the other on the train.

When you wake up in the morning
asking, "What's your name?"
And I roll over toward your pillow
saying, "Don't play games."

And we're staring out the window
at the down-pouring rain.
We see a blind man cross the road
and drop his cane.

That's the way we are,
and now I know our love's in vain
when you got one foot on the platform,
and the other on the train.

IT RAINED
August 5, 2014

It rained and it rained and it rained and it rained
and it rained and it rained some more.
It rained and it rained 'til the ground got wet
then it rained and it rained some more.

Coffee tastes like bitter tears,
but it rained and it rained some more.
It rained and it rained 'til the ground got wet
then it rained and it rained some more.

I could sleep for a thousand years,
but it rained and it rained some more.
It rained and it rained 'til the ground got wet
then it rained and it rained some more.

But sleep brings ruthless nightmares
that drag you to the floor.
It rained and it rained 'til the ground got wet,
then it rained and it rained some more.

While waking up brings horrors
that it never did before.
It rained and it rained 'til the ground got wet,
then it rained and it rained some more.

What do you do when death's cold fist
is knocking at your door?
It rained and it rained 'til the ground got wet,
then it rained and it rained some more.

And all that love just drifts away
so far from your heart's shore?
It rained and it rained 'til the ground got wet,
then it rained and it rained some more.

Driving away from that mountaintop
it rained but'll rain some more.
It rained and it rained 'til the ground got wet,
then it rained and it rained some more.

Roll in grass that's wet and hot,
it rained but will rain some more.
It rained and it rained 'til the ground got wet,
then it rained and it rained some more.

It rained and it rained and it rained and it rained
and it rained and it rained some more.
It rained and it rained 'til the ground got wet
and it was a sweet release.

FEBRUARY 14th

Dave tells me how he's gonna spend Valentine's Day.
It seems he will wait up all night if necessary
so that he can bait and catch a bristle worm
that resides in his pride-and-joy fishtank:
A smelly, unwelcome tenant.

The worm hides in the rocks at the bottom of the tank
and can stretch up to three feet long,
and it bites chunks out of his sea anemones.

Dave says the bristle worm is also known as the fire worm
because if you have the misfortune to touch the spikes
that adorn its spine,
it'll bring back memories of receiving tattoos.

I am angry now.
That little fucker worm!
How dare he invade Dave's fish tank—
A place of peace, and beauty?
How dare he bite chunks out of Dave's sea anemones?
How dare he make Dave's finger throb,
red-hot to the touch?

Dave has patience.
He has waited one year
until the time was right to catch the worm.
Tonight, he will sit for hours,
alert in the deafening darkness,
awaiting the nemesis
who makes his slimy stage debut
only when after-hours bars are open.

Dave is mysterious and private—
Qualities I've always admired,
but never seemed to be able to achieve, myself.

He won't tell anyone his age.
He believes in capital punishment,
and his child is his fish tank.

Dave promises me that
when he catches that bristle worm tonight,
he's gonna put it in a jar and show it to me.

I am honored, blessed—
Hey, I'm no fool.
Through experience, I have learned
to recognize angels when they appear to me.
I never refuse their gifts,
and I always pick them up hitchhiking.

E. D. Evans

THE BOY FROM HELL

Most girls like a boy who is dandy and swell,
But not me—My Prince Charming is AWOL from Hell.
The lines on his face are as deep as a well.
Yeah, I know that boy, and he comes straight from Hell.

He creeps 'round the corner at night in my dreams.
He drifts up my legs through my stockings and seams.
He covets my mind—Now I'm under his spell.
How I want that boy who has travelled from Hell.

Cleans his teeth with a switchblade
while whistling the blues,
scars everywhere, and arms full of tattoos.
Though some girls like boys who are dandy and swell,
not me, Man, my boy took the last flight from Hell.

He crawls through my nightmares, I'm losing my sleep.
He whispers and kisses, he slinks and he creeps.
His soul is the only thing left he can't sell.
Oh, I want that boy who has come straight from Hell.

Multiple earrings and eyes like a snake's,
broken-toothed smile that quivers and quakes,
raspy-assed voice that could set off a bell:
That's my boy, I know him, and his passport's from Hell.

I searched for him everywhere, holding my net,
took my turn at the Black Jack and spun the Roulette.
It was Satan who told me that I won that bet.
Our Hells were both here, and it's here that we met.

He spews needles and pins and cries out in his dreams.
He rants and he raves and he shouts and he screams.
We're together at last, think we'll sit for a spell,
and the postcards we'll send you say: *Greetings, From Hell!*

JACKAL, THE CONJUROR

The train took Jackal to a cobblestone square
filled with Parisian aromas of spices and gin.
Young white flamingos graced Alsatian lands,
feathers not yet pink stinking of carnal sin.

Just like English Leather—That musky teen scent,
waiting to turn those white feathers to pink.
Under blue waters shrimp swam in repent,
ready to rise, yet more able to sink.

Jackal, the beauty, smokes John Players at dawn
while young white flamingos in their gilded cages
stretch translucent wings, and then stifle a yawn,
taking nearly-pink pauses from one-legged rages.

She muses on how their bills have yet to curve.
She muses on why they have yet to turn pink.
She muses on what gilded cages must hold,
and that shrimp will not rise when it's past time to sink.

She muses on when English Leather was King.
She muses on where she placed that photo album.
She muses on thoughts both profound and obscene,
yet believes thoughts like these are nothing but pablum.

These are the tall tales that our souls etch in ink.
These are the words that we daren't repeat,
from the top of our boiled brains, brought to the brink
of the soles of our aching, misanthropic feet.

Stop now or this forever-ever poem will welcome chaos,
and if that's the case, we've come aways now, haven't we?
As if joy can be reduced to a megaton albatross,
and white flamingos await in all their pink vanity.

PART V
EASTERN BALLADS

LONDONTOWN

Boots and glory, Londontown,
Old Union Jack and leather.
A man can only count on change—
Nowt stays the same forever.

Trite as shite as it might sound,
that is how we hit the ground,
reckless punks in DM boots
and trendy mods in skinny suits.

Got pissed at after-hours pubs
when the filth was on the beat.
They smashed us with their billy clubs—
Then, Londontown was not so sweet.

Black and white skanked arm-in-arm
to reggae, ska, and dub's hot scene.
But skins turned into racist pigs
committing violent acts obscene.

Margaret Thatcher made life hell,
Despair raged down an endless hole.
No jobs around, my friends were skint,
signing on to get their dole.

The boys were hard, the girls were tough,
romance did not exist.
We slammed to tunes while garage bands
spat at us to Resist.

We broke squats on the Loughborough Road
and lived from day-to-day.
Brick alleys smelled of piss and chips
and curry take-away.

We were not Hippie Boomers—
We were Generation Jones.
Speed and smack insomniacs
who worshipped dust and bones.

There's not much left to speak about
that hasn't yet been said.
So many of us from that scene
are fucked, sober, or dead.

At night, the two-tone sirens wail
their ancient, vacant sound
for all the Rastas, Punks, and Scooter Mods
who once ruled Londontown.

EAST VILLAGE TWELVE-STEPPING, 1980s

The new ultimate cool can be found downtown
drinking cups of coffee on St. Marks Place,
where you can hip-hop into any 12-step meeting
and confess your shamed disgrace.
There, you can find an excuse to justify
your antisocial action.
Hold those in contempt
that may be exempt
from your new-found sobriety faction.

Downtown all the heroes are
no living saints.
They sit at their bar stools
showing off self-restraint
and drink seltzer and juice.
Their egos intact.
Their tongues aren't loose.
They're facing this fact.
They've crawled out of the gutter.
Their life's in a box—
But still wish they were drinking
scotch on the rocks.

Their friends pretend awe,
but under their breath say,
"Glad it's not me.
I'd rather face death."

"You don't understand,"
the sinners will say,
tossing hair out of eyes
and sauntering away.

"You were never a dysfunctional
obsessive-compulsive/sado-masochistic/
adult child of an alcoholic.
You never blacked out for ten solid years.
You can't understand my angst and my fears."

No, I don't understand
all those years that you fled
from the bowels of pain
while I sat there in dread,
knowing full well I'd be burned with a brand,
not escaping in drink when things got out of hand.

Are you AA, OA, NA, or an AC of A?
What childhood trauma's causing stress for today,
helping you linger and watching you stray,
and is making you speak in this alien way?

Then, "Easy does it."
"God is my co-pilot."
You're truly downtown funky.
"One day at a time" is fine,
but don't show me contempt
like I'm some laboratory monkey.
Remember just to "Think, think, think."
Speak a new sober lingo instead of downing that drink.
"Denial's not just a river in Egypt."
Remain cool all the while,
now it's dysfunctional-hip, Bohemian style.

(Continued)

No more endless nights of throwing up
and falling down the stairs.
No more nodding at the club,
forgetting all your cares.

Twelve-step meetings are the place to be,
replacing human intimacy.
They give you a God.
You relinquish all choice
as you give yourself up
to the twelve-stepping voice.

Now I have no objection to anyone
fighting for sobriety.
I just can't stand the attitude
of false, clean, holy piety,
and those who think they're the only ones
who've been through living hell.
Fools rush in and take a seat
where wise men fear to dwell.

Those who believe no one else can know pain
who isn't a drunk or a junkie,
who think they're alone in this troublesome vein—
The utmost cool and funky.

I've been excluded, I can't understand.
I'm not in that sacred garage band
of downtown, sober twelve-steppers
who shun and ridicule
because I'd rather live my life outside any program
than in meetings with the ultimate cool.

AVENUE B

Through the bleached-blonde palladium
of musky racketeers,
through the jaunted, jaded memories
piled high like souvenirs,
the speedless nights
the nightless speed
all cried without a cost.
Vaporized by silence,
only love alone was lost.

The black-look leather
smelled of dirty danger done.
The darkest circles under eyes
weren't hidden by the sun.
The smell of sweat, and septic "Thanks"
were hidden by disguise in the
Glade-Solid toilet tanks revealed behind her eyes.

And she laughed at broken promises
and serpent-tongued guise.
Into the night she broke despite the
dirt, disgust, and lies.

Stony, sitting open-mouthed at what she had to tell,
he felt himself transformed into another space, or Hell,
and the cheap, cheap, gazes of the people so unkind
turned his mind into a maze
and amaze into his mind.
And it hurt so very badly
but he loved her anyway
while a strong but silent reckoning
sifts all that pain away.

NO STOPPING THE JUICE

The trial of the century
on NBC and ABC and CNN and CBS
was one unholy fucking mess.

Game Six, The Finals, Jordan's gone—
He's playing baseball badly.
New York City's crazed with hope,
but the Rockets defend madly.
The New York Knicks are dreaming "Ring"—
Fourth quarter left to dance.
If Riley's sure of anything,
it's Ewing's final chance.

The screen goes black
and when it's back,
I can't believe my eyes.
It ain't Hakeem Olajuwan
shot-blocking for the prize.
Instead, a white Ford Bronco
that is cruising 55.
A fugitive in the making,
OJ: *Wanted Dead or Alive.*

And so began an escapade
shoved in the nation's face,
of murder, sex, cocaine, and wealth,
not Oakley, Starks, and Mase.
The drama on the Garden floor
would only serve to taunt us
while the drama in the courtroom
was what truly came to haunt us.

Marcia Clarke, with poodly-hair,
was trying to save face.
When would the public realize
they were trying class, not race?
And Mister Johnny Cochran
whose rant was never-ending:
"If the glove don't fit, you must acquit!"
So smug and condescending.

A year-long trial then OJ's free—
Just a quick deliberation.
No longer would we see his mug
on every TV station.
And one would think this would be cause
for manic celebration.
Instead, a great racial divide
and, *What price, liberation?*

The Knicks went on to lose, of course.
(That was money in the bank.)
Eight million hopes were quickly dashed,
Eight million hearts that sank.
If Starks had just maintained his cool
and stopped blasting those threes,
and Ewing hadn't worn out
all the cartilage in his knees,
then Harper was a shoo-in
for Defensive MVP.

So, OJ moved from Rockingham,
ex-idol of the masses.
Forever gone, those glory days
of touchdowns, blocks, and passes.
And somewhere Ron says to Nicole,
"Here—Take your fucking glasses."

E. D. Evans

GONE NEW YORK GONE NEW YORK GONE

Heartless calculating deals run
Bread and Circus entertainment.
Nothing's new under the dome.
The payoff's not in self-containment.

No salary caps for cell-phone suits,
deals at midnight, drool on loot.
Indentured service is this sport—
On and off the hardwood court.

Mid-air arc to metal mouth,
fishnet dangling below.
Swoosh means "Money"
North and South.
Garden egos grow and grow.

Bang and clang and hug the rim,
spin again and topple in.
Yes—Success—That's how you do it!
Glass hoop, bloody dunk
smashing through it.

It's not about the game (small g).
It's all about the Game (Big G).
Wall Street gangsters' stocks and sales,
phat endorsements fly or fail.
City Dancers shake their teats
for rich boys far from nose-bleed seats.

What was once spectacular
is corporate vernacular,
and now a different Aesop's fable
whose moral lies in memories,
blinding me with costly cable,
Get it LIVE on MSG!

I used to think that when I died
and threw in the last towel,
the five words on my tombstone would read:
"It counts . . . and the foul!"

Man was I wrong,
Those days are gone—
That ain't no more my kicks.
I used to live and breathe that game—
Now goodbye, New York Knicks.

E. D. Evans

NOWT/NAUGHT

It took a long time for naught to be born.
There was naught in the night-time
and naught in the morn.
There was naught from the critters buried deeply in sand.
There was naught for the nail in the palm of my hand.

Then a time never passed where naught wasn't key.
It was naught for the wasp and naught for the bee.
It was naught for the sinner and naught for the saint.
It was naught for the hearty and naught for the faint.

Naught was left over for supper tomorrow—
Naught to be salvaged or stolen or borrowed.
Naught could be said about yourself or me.
Naught was a rustler strung up a tall tree.

There was naught for your Monday,
and naught by the door.
There was naught for your Tuesday,
smashed bits on the floor.

There was naught for your Wednesday,
and naught for your tea.
There was naught but the rage
that lay cold, silently.

There was naught on a Thursday, and Friday, dry too.
There was naught for the old maid
trapped dead in her shoe.
There was naught on that Saturday. Sunday was quiet.
And whatever you're selling, well, naught wouldn't buy it.

The days passed by quickly and naught was the same,
notorious naught running wild, not tame.
In the blink of an eye, life had passed by,
and naught was to blame for its passage, but I.

RECTIFY

Do not go into the barn,
for a noose is strung high
on a rafter in there.
Its gape will lie low 'neath the line of your jaw.
Matters not if its song is righteous or fair.

Now your fate lies with owls that hoot in the night
and a noose hanging high in that barn.
A snap of a neck bone stretched out oh-so-tight,
a blackout and POOF—You are gone.

So, now, rectify all in your heart and head
the ones you love most before you are dead.